LADYBIRD  HISTORIES

Second World War

History consultant: Terry Charman, Imperial War Museum, London
Map illustrator: Martin Sanders

LADYBIRD BOOKS

UK | USA | Canada | Ireland | Australia
India | New Zealand | South Africa

Ladybird Books is part of the Penguin Random House group of companies
whose addresses can be found at global.penguinrandomhouse.com.

www.penguin.co.uk   www.puffin.co.uk   www.ladybird.co.uk

First published 2014
002

Copyright © Ladybird Books Ltd, 2014

Printed and bound in Hong Kong

A CIP catalogue record for this book is available from the British Library

ISBN: 978–0–723–27727–9

All correspondence to
Ladybird Books
Penguin Random House Children's Books
80 Strand, London WC2R 0RL

LADYBIRD HISTORIES

Second World War

Written by Simon Adams
Main illustrations by Nick Hardcastle
Cartoon illustrations by Clive Goodyer

Contents

Introduction

In 1939, a war broke out in Europe that within two years had spread around the world. Huge battles were fought on land, at sea and in the air. By the time the war ended six years later in 1945, many millions of people had lost their lives. Millions more had been made homeless. We call this terrible event the Second World War.

After the First World War

The First World War had ended 21 years before, in 1918. Britain, France, Russia and the United States of America (USA) fought on one side and Germany and Austria-Hungary on the other. The war ended with defeat for Germany. The Treaty of Versailles ended the war and many Germans considered the penalties it imposed to be very harsh on their country. In 1933, a new party and its leader promised to overthrow the treaty and make Germany strong again.

EUROPE IN 1939

Germany and Italy

Adolf Hitler and his Nazi Party believed in a strong government and wanted to increase Germany's military strength. Hitler also believed that the German people were better than anyone else in the world. In particular, he hated Jews. Hitler became a dictator and crushed all opposition to his rule. He built up the armed forces and took over both Austria and what is now the Czech Republic. Hitler wanted to create a new German Reich, or empire, in Europe. All these actions went against the treaty that had ended the First World War.

In 1936, Germany formed a partnership with Italy, whose ruler, Benito Mussolini, wanted to expand Italian power around the Mediterranean Sea. In 1939, the two countries signed an alliance known as the Pact of Steel. Britain and France objected to Germany and Italy's actions and formed their own alliance to stop them.

Mussolini (left) supported Hitler (right) because he thought it would help Italy to expand as a European power.

The Road to War in Asia

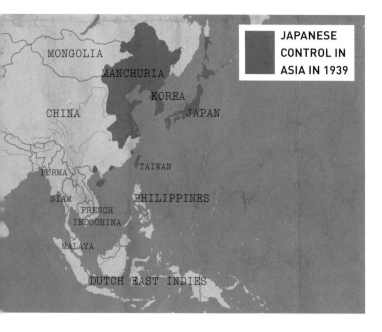

JAPANESE CONTROL IN ASIA IN 1939

MONGOLIA
MANCHURIA
KOREA
CHINA
JAPAN
BURMA
TAIWAN
SIAM
PHILIPPINES
FRENCH INDOCHINA
MALAYA
DUTCH EAST INDIES

On the other side of the world Japan, too, was preparing for war. Japan had fought with the British against Germany in the First World War. Like the Germans, it also did not like the Treaty of Versailles as it had gained very few new lands to rule. Japan felt that it had not been rewarded enough for its victory.

In the years leading up to the Second World War, Japan was keen to show the world its expanding military power.

Military leadership

The emperor of Japan was head of the country, but real power lay with the military leaders. They believed in a strong Japan and wanted to create a vast Japanese empire in eastern Asia. Japan had few natural resources of its own and it wanted to control overseas supplies, such as oil, coal, iron and rubber. Japan already ruled Korea and Taiwan. In 1931, it seized the resource-rich Chinese province of Manchuria. Six years later, in 1937, Japan invaded the rest of China. It also later took over French colonies in south-east Asia.

In 1936, Japan signed a treaty with Germany. By 1940, they had signed the Axis Pact with Italy. These three countries were determined to divide and rule the world between them.

The Start of the War

The Treaty of Versailles gave the newly independent country of Poland a strip of land through Germany. This allowed it access to the Baltic Sea. Germany wanted the land back and it threatened Poland with war if it refused to hand it over. Britain and France were alarmed and promised that they would declare war on Germany if it invaded Poland.

The Nazi–Soviet Pact

Before Germany invaded, it wanted to be sure that Poland was not supported by the Union of Soviet Socialist Republics (USSR), the empire that Russia was part of. In 1939, Germany signed an agreement with Russia that allowed it to invade western Poland. The Soviet Union would then occupy eastern Poland and other areas along its western border.

The German blitzkrieg attacks were first launched against Poland, then Belgium, Luxembourg and the Netherlands.

Invasion of Poland

On 1 September 1939, German forces crossed the border into Poland. Two days later, Britain and France declared war on Germany. On 17 September, the Soviet Union occupied eastern Poland. After a period of heavy bombing by Germany, Poland surrendered at the end of the month. The Second World War had begun.

Blitzkrieg

The German armies attacked Poland with a blitzkrieg, a German word meaning 'lightning war'. Columns of tanks and other armoured vehicles, supported by aerial bombers, rapidly advanced into the country. A shortened version of the word – 'blitz' – referred to the aerial attacks that Germany launched against London in 1940–41.

The Phoney War

After the invasion of Poland, peace returned to Europe. This period was known as the phoney war because no major fighting actually took place. An exception to this was in Finland, which the Soviet Union attacked in order to gain military bases and create a strong border around Leningrad (now St Petersburg).

Preparations for war

All the countries at war stepped up their plans. They produced new guns, tanks and warplanes, and added more men to their armies. At home, the civilian population also got ready for war. Air-raid shelters were dug to protect citizens from bombing attacks. In Britain, every man, woman and child was given a gas mask in case the Germans used poison gas in an attack. There were many false alarms during the phoney war and none of the shelters were used in an actual air raid.

Taking shelter

Anderson shelters were built in most British city gardens. They were made from corrugated iron, dug into the ground and then covered with earth. Later, an indoor version, called the Morrison shelter, was introduced for people without gardens. Public air-raid shelters were built in parks and other places.

Evacuation

Many British children were evacuated from the big towns and cities so that they were safe from bombing. Some were sent to live with new families in the countryside. Most children missed their own families and were scared of the cows and other animals in the fields, which they had never seen before. But as the phoney war continued some children were brought home again, as it seemed that the real war would never start.

Some children travelled by train to their temporary homes in the countryside.

The Fall of France

The end of the phoney war came suddenly. In April 1940, German troops swept north through Denmark and into Norway. Britain, France and Poland sent troops to defend Norway, but it was too late. The real war had begun.

A new government

In Britain, Neville Chamberlain resigned as prime minister on 10 May 1940. His successor was Winston Churchill. On the same day, German troops attacked France and trapped the British Army. A fleet of ships evacuated the troops from the beaches at Dunkirk and ferried them back across the English Channel to Britain. This was called Operation Dynamo.

Over 330,000 troops were rescued at Dunkirk during Operation Dynamo. A fleet of 'small ships' – privately owned pleasure boats or fishing vessels – carried 27,000 of them to safety.

Heading to Paris

German troops entered Paris, the French capital, on 14 June 1940 and forced France to surrender. Germany now occupied northern and western France. A new French government agreed an armistice with Germany and ruled the south of the country from the town of Vichy. The French general, Charles de Gaulle, fled to London. He successfully rallied resistance to the German occupation with the Free French movement.

Hitler and his generals visited Paris just nine days after the Nazis took control of the city.

A global war

At the end of June, German troops occupied the Channel Islands. These were the only parts of Britain's territory that were occupied during the war. Earlier that month, Italy had joined the war on the German side. It occupied parts of southern France and attacked British colonies in east Africa. The European war was becoming a global conflict.

The Battle of Britain

After the fall of France in 1940, Britain and its empire stood alone against Germany. Winston Churchill said that Britain would fight on against Germany. 'We shall never surrender,' he said. The Germans prepared to invade Britain from the sea in Operation Sea Lion. First though, they had to gain total control of the skies.

Fighting in the sky

On 10 July 1940, squadrons of German dive bombers attacked a convoy of ships in the English Channel. In the following days, German Messerschmitt fighters and Dornier bombers attacked British harbours, ships and military and aircraft bases. They wanted to defeat the Royal Air Force (RAF) and take control of the skies above Britain. In response, British Hurricane and Spitfire fighters took to the air to attack the incoming German planes and shoot them down. Brave pilots fought each other in aerial dogfights. This became known as the Battle of Britain. Many pilots lost their lives and many planes were shot down.

The 'few'

The Battle of Britain raged on until 31 October. By then, the Germans had lost too many planes and pilots, so the battle was called off. The Royal Air Force had won. Winston Churchill said that 'never in the field of human conflict was so much owed by so many to so few.'

The Supermarine Spitfire was the fastest fighter aircraft in the Royal Air Force, but the Hawker Hurricane (centre of the picture below) was responsible for more German losses.

The Blitz

Even before the Battle of Britain ended, Germany began a new campaign to defeat Britain – the Blitz. On 7 September 1940, German bombers attacked London. Over 1,000 people were killed or injured, while homes and factories were wrecked.

Terror from the skies

The Blitz was terrifying. As bombs rained down from the skies, people rushed into the underground shelters for protection. The Germans wanted to destroy British cities and frighten the country into surrendering. One of the worst attacks took place on 14 November 1940 when German bombers bombed Coventry, destroying the old cathedral. The Blitz ended in May 1941 when Hitler turned his attention towards the Soviet Union. However, later in the war, Germany fired V-1 flying bombs and V-2 rockets at Britain, killing even more people.

Air-raid wardens

The ARP (Air Raid Precautions) wardens carried out important tasks during the Blitz, such as sounding the air-raid sirens and helping people move safely to and from the shelters. They were often the first to arrive at a bomb site, attending to casualties and organizing emergency help. Both men and women worked as air-raid wardens and the vast majority were volunteers.

During the Blitz, firefighters put out fires caused by the bombing raids. But the next day, even as buildings continued to burn, people carried on with their normal lives.

Bombing Germany

Britain and its allies fought back by bombing German cities. In May 1942, 1,000 British bombers destroyed the old German city of Cologne, while further nightly raids flattened many other towns and cities. Two large dams in the Ruhr Valley were blown up with special 'bouncing bombs'.
In February 1945, 25,000 civilians were killed when a bombing raid caused a massive fire in Dresden.

The Home Front

The war was not just fought by the military abroad. It was also fought by ordinary people at home. Day after day they had to cope with enemy air attacks, find enough food to eat and get to and from work. Above all, they had to keep their spirits up and believe that their country would win the war. The experience of the war by civilians became known as the 'Home Front'.

Rationing

The war changed everything. Food brought in from abroad, such as sugar, tea, bacon and meat, was rationed because it was too dangerous and difficult to bring such goods to Britain by sea. Bananas and other foreign fruits disappeared completely. In Britain, people were asked to 'Dig For Victory', growing their own vegetables in their gardens and allotments. Petrol, too, was in very short supply, so few people were able to drive cars or vans. Road signs were also removed in case an invading army made use of them.

Ration books

In Britain, people were issued with ration books and queued to get their weekly allowance of food. As well as other rations, everyone was given 50g (2oz) of tea and one egg per week. Sausages were of such poor quality that people called them 'breadcrumbs in battledress'. Everyone was a little hungry, but no one starved during the war.

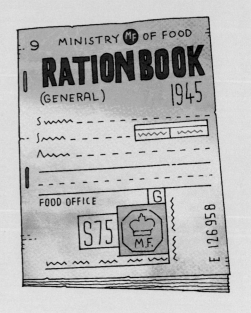

The blackout

When evening came everybody had to put up blackout curtains to make sure no light shone through their windows. Streetlights were also switched off throughout the war. Any light visible from the sky might have helped enemy bombers find a target to bomb.

People entertained themselves at home during the blackout. They listened to the radio for news of the war and enjoyed the shows that were broadcast.

Women at War

The Second World War is sometimes called a 'total war' because both troops and civilians were involved. Women played a major role and took up jobs. The war could not have been fought without the important contribution made by women.

Working women

Before the war many women did not work. But when war broke out they were required to fill the jobs the men had left behind when they went to war. Many women worked in factories producing weapons and machines. In Britain, some women joined auxiliary or support services for the military. They mended engines, worked as code-breakers and flew planes to where they were needed. Many also became nurses or drove ambulances. In Russia, some women even joined the army.

Some British women joined the Women's Land Army and worked on farms as 'Land Girls'. Others joined the Timber Corps and cut down trees for wood. These women were known as 'Lumberjills'.

Children at War

Children's lives were totally disrupted by the war. School lessons often stopped when there was an air-raid warning and many schools were bombed. Favourite foods were rationed or disappeared altogether. Few people had a proper summer holiday. In Britain, the beaches were closed off with barbed wire to prevent German troops landing. The war was frightening and it brought sadness for many children. Some children were killed and many more lost their parents.

Children were told to carry their gas masks with them at all times and were taught how to put them on quickly. Some gas masks were made in bright colours.

Evacuees leaving their homes wore labels that said where they were being sent. To leave family behind was very upsetting for most children.

Bomb sites were often used as playgrounds by children. They played games, pretended to be soldiers and searched for souvenirs of the war. This was very dangerous.

There were not many toys because the materials were needed to make machines and weapons. Toys were often made at home from wood and paper.

War in the Atlantic

Throughout the war, a deadly battle took place in the North Atlantic Ocean as Germany attempted to starve Britain out of the war. German bombers attacked from the air and U-boats patrolled the seas, hunting down and sinking ships that belonged to Britain and its allies.

The convoy system

In order to survive the war, Britain needed to bring in weapons, oil, food and other much-needed supplies. These were carried across the North Atlantic in merchant ships. The ships sailed together in convoys that were protected by large naval warships. The convoys often changed course to confuse the enemy. Despite this tactic, the ships were often attacked by German U-boats.

Convoys of ships crossed the North Atlantic at the speed of the slowest ship in the group. This meant they were very vulnerable to attack. Many sailors lost their lives.

Success and defeat

The U-boats were very successful at first. They sank 3,500 merchant ships and 175 warships. But the British fought back. In 1941, British warships were fitted with radar that could detect a U-boat on the surface up to 9 kilometres (6 miles) away. The British also managed to read German naval messages. This allowed them to understand the German plans and redirect convoys away from the U-boats. Eventually the British Navy won, sinking 783 U-boats. More than 30,000 German sailors lost their lives.

The U-boats

German Unterseeboote (undersea boats) hunted Allied ships in packs. They fired their torpedoes while on the surface and then dived deep into the ocean to protect themselves from attack by enemy aircraft.

Operation Barbarossa

GERMAN LINES OF ADVANCE INTO THE USSR, 1941

Adolf Hitler did not like the Soviet Union. He considered the Russians to be 'subhumans' and hated their communist system of government. One of his aims in the war was to defeat the USSR and wipe it off the face of the earth.

In late 1940, Germany prepared to invade the USSR. To do this, it needed support from the Balkan countries. Hungary, Bulgaria and Romania all offered support, but Yugoslavia refused and was invaded; so, too, was Greece. With these new allies, Germany could launch Operation Barbarossa against the USSR.

Caught by surprise

The USSR became an ally of Britain when, on 22 June 1941, a massive German army of 3.6 million soldiers, with 3,600 tanks and 2,700 aircraft crossed the Soviet border. The Soviets were caught by surprise – most of their aircraft were destroyed. In September 1941 more than 600,000 Red Army soldiers were killed or captured. One enormous German army headed north to Leningrad, while another advanced east towards the capital, Moscow. A third headed south to capture the oilfields of the Caucasus. By winter, German troops had conquered most of the western USSR and were camped outside Moscow.

On 15 September 1941, German troops and their Finnish allies surrounded Leningrad. The city remained under siege for more than two years and many people starved to death. The siege finally ended on 19 January 1944.

Pearl Harbor

The USA had been concerned about the war in Europe. Though it did not want to fight, neither did it want Germany and Italy to win. The USA therefore lent ships, arms and other support to the British. Across the Pacific Ocean, Japan continued to expand its empire. With no warning, Japan attacked the US naval base at Pearl Harbor in Hawaii on 7 December 1941. The USA had no choice but to join the war.

A truly global war

In an attempt to prevent Japanese expansion in Asia, the USA, Britain and the Dutch East Indies (now Indonesia) had cut most of the supply of oil to Japan. In response, Japan attacked Pearl Harbor to try to gain control of the Pacific. As allies of Japan, Germany and Italy declared war on the USA, too. The USA joined the war as an ally of Britain and the USSR. The war had truly become a world war.

Quick conquests

Just a few days after Pearl Harbor, Japanese troops attacked the US-controlled Philippines, British Malaya, Borneo and Burma, and the Dutch East Indies. The British colony of Hong Kong in China fell to the Japanese on Christmas Day and the important British naval base of Singapore fell in February 1942. Japan now controlled the whole of south-east Asia.

Nineteen ships were destroyed and 2,403 sailors lost their lives in the attack on Pearl Harbor. US President Roosevelt described it as a 'date which will live in infamy'.

Battle of Midway

After their successes in south-east Asia, the Japanese seized islands across the Pacific Ocean. In April 1942, a Japanese fleet headed south through the Solomon Islands to attack Port Moresby in New Guinea. From there, Japan would be able to dominate northern Australia and perhaps capture the entire country.

The Coral Sea

In May 1942, the US and Japanese fleets arrived in the Coral Sea to the north-east of Australia. The two fleets of aircraft carriers and other ships were so far apart that they never saw each other. Attacking from the air, the Americans sank all three Japanese carriers and stopped the Japanese advance towards Australia. Four weeks later, a US fleet stopped the Japanese invasion of an important military base on Midway Island in the North Pacific.

Operation Cartwheel

After the Battle of Midway the US had the advantage.
It defeated Japan in New Guinea and managed to recapture
the important island of Guadalcanal in the Solomon Islands.
In June 1943, they launched Operation Cartwheel, hopping
from island to island to remove the Japanese. Meanwhile
Britain, assisted by troops from its empire, fought a difficult
war against the Japanese in Burma.

The Battle of Midway was the first battle to be fought using planes
flying from aircraft carriers to attack enemy ships.

War in Africa

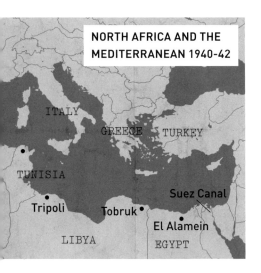

NORTH AFRICA AND THE MEDITERRANEAN 1940-42

ITALY
GREECE
TURKEY
TUNISIA
Tripoli
Tobruk
Suez Canal
El Alamein
LIBYA
EGYPT

Italy declared war on Britain in June 1940. Troops from the Italian colony of Libya then attacked British-run Egypt and the Suez Canal, which was an important shipping route. The British quickly pushed the Italians back into Libya. They also expelled the army from Ethiopia and their colonies in East Africa. Faced with probable defeat, Hitler sent General Rommel to support the Italians.

El Alamein

Erwin Rommel was a brilliant general. He pushed the British back towards Egypt and surrounded the city of Tobruk in April 1941. The battle raged back and forth until Tobruk fell to the Germans in June 1942. The Germans then advanced towards the canal. The British 8th Army, led by General Montgomery, faced them at El Alamein in Egypt. Fighting lasted from 23 October to 8 November. Victory gave Britain a major boost in the war and the successful troops then pushed Rommel back into Libya.

The Desert Rats

The 7th Armoured Division fought as part of the British 8th Army in north Africa. They became known as the Desert Rats because of their cunning and their ability to survive in the harsh desert.

Operation Torch

On the other side of Africa, American and British troops began Operation Torch. They landed in north-west Africa and pushed east. The two Allied armies met in Tunisia and in May 1943 forced the surrender of the German and Italian armies. North Africa was secure; the Allies could now turn their attention to Europe once more.

Over 55,000 American and British troops in tanks and other armoured vehicles invaded north-west Africa during Operation Torch.

Stalingrad

During 1942, German troops pushed deep into the USSR. In August, they attacked the important city of Stalingrad on the River Volga. The city was named after the Soviet leader, Josef Stalin, and had symbolic importance for the Soviet people. To capture it would be a major prize for the Germans and neither side was prepared to give up easily.

Building-to-building combat

At first, the Germans appeared to have won. They forced the Red Army into a narrow strip of buildings along the west bank of the river and besieged them. Snipers shot at each other from building to building and sometimes from floor to floor inside the same building. Both sides lost many men.

Counter-attack

In November, the Red Army set up a counter-attack around the back of the German lines and surrounded the German troops. The besieging forces were now besieged themselves. The battle continued through the cold winter until the Germans surrendered in February 1943.

The significance of Stalingrad

Stalingrad was a major defeat for the Germans and an important victory for the Soviets. From now on, the Red Army took control and gradually pushed the Germans out of the USSR.

The fight for Stalingrad lasted five months and ten days. More than 1 million Axis troops and 1,140,000 Soviet troops took part. Perhaps 750,000 Axis troops were killed, wounded or went missing; about 480,000 Soviets were killed and another 650,000 wounded.

Under Occupation

For much of the war, large parts of Europe, eastern Asia and Africa were under enemy occupation. Entire countries disappeared from the map completely. Others were ruled by governors put in place by the occupying country.

Hard times

Throughout Europe, resistance to German and Italian rule was crushed. Political parties were banned and meetings broken up. In some occupied countries, it was forbidden to own or even listen to the radio. A curfew every night kept people in their homes. The Germans forced large numbers of prisoners of war to work as labourers in Germany. These men dug for coal and worked in factories and on farms. In the Far East, the Japanese were particularly cruel to those they conquered.

Prisoners of war

Both sides in the war took thousands of prisoners. The International Red Cross sent prisoners food parcels and delivered letters from home. The Germans treated British prisoners of war reasonably well in order to make sure their own prisoners in Britain received good treatment, too. Both Germany and the USSR treated each other's prisoners very badly; poor conditions meant many of them died before the end of the war.

Allied officers that tried to escape from prison camps were sent to Colditz Castle in eastern Germany.

Colditz

Colditz Castle was meant to be escape-proof but, over the course of the war, sixty prisoners did manage to flee using a number of ingenious plans. One Scottish prisoner was smuggled out inside a straw mattress, while six Dutch officers escaped through a manhole cover in the exercise yard.

Collaboration and Resistance

Across occupied Europe and Asia, some people welcomed the Germans, Italians or Japanese and collaborated with them. Others rose up in resistance against them.

Collaboration

Across Europe, many people worked for the Germans and supported them. In unoccupied Vichy France, Marshal Petain and his government actively collaborated with Germany. So, too, did the governments of Croatia, Slovakia, Hungary and Romania. While in Norway the former war minister, Vidkun Quisling, took power as a Nazi sympathizer. The situation in Asia was different as most places Japan conquered were European or American colonies. Many people here welcomed the Japanese as fellow Asians freeing them from foreign rule. The Japanese supported local governments and allowed Burma and the Philippines some independence.

Resistance

Despite official collaboration, resistance to German rule quickly spread. Resistance groups formed in France, Norway and elsewhere. In Yugoslavia, and behind German lines in the USSR, large-scale partisan armies fought the Germans. They achieved great success. In 1944, partisan armies liberated both Yugoslavia and Albania from German rule.

The French Resistance disrupted the German war effort as much as it could.
The sabotage of trains and railway lines was a common method of attack.

Undercover Operations

All nations in the war needed to know what their enemy was doing. This intelligence was provided by spies. Spying was a dangerous activity. If spies were caught, they would be shot.

Spying

Britain, Germany and the USSR had large spy networks. Spies sent home information about enemy troop movements and other activities. They also provided information on industrial and military targets that could be bombed from the air. In 1940, the British set up the Special Operations Executive (SOE) to gather intelligence from occupied Europe and to carry out operations abroad. In May 1942, the SOE supported the Czech Resistance when it killed Reinhard Heydrich, the Nazi ruler of the country. But not all the information spies sent back was believed. In 1941, Soviet leader Josef Stalin did not accept intelligence that suggested Germany was about to invade his country, Russia.

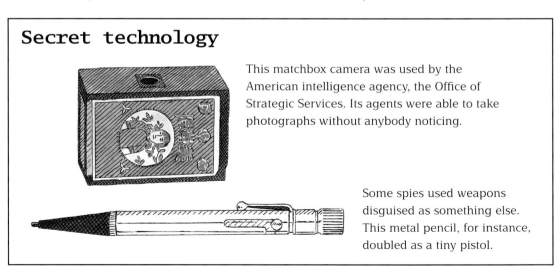

Secret technology

This matchbox camera was used by the American intelligence agency, the Office of Strategic Services. Its agents were able to take photographs without anybody noticing.

Some spies used weapons disguised as something else. This metal pencil, for instance, doubled as a tiny pistol.

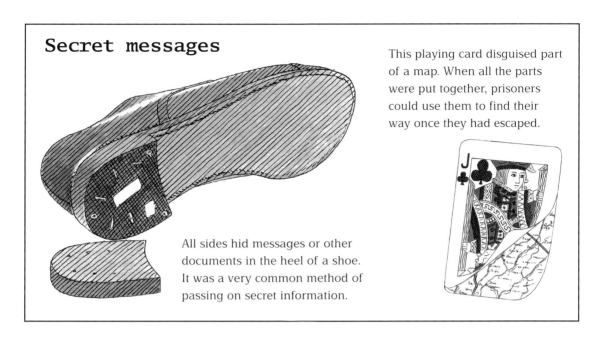

Secret messages

This playing card disguised part of a map. When all the parts were put together, prisoners could use them to find their way once they had escaped.

All sides hid messages or other documents in the heel of a shoe. It was a very common method of passing on secret information.

The Enigma Code

All sides sent military messages in code. The Germans sent their messages through a code machine called Enigma. Agents working at the British code-breaking centre, Bletchley Park, were able to discover how Enigma worked. They could then understand Germany's secret messages. This success provided valuable information about the location of German U-boats and troops.

Important code

The Germans were sure that Enigma was safe. Throughout the war they never knew that the British had broken its codes and were reading all their messages. Breaking Enigma saved thousands of Allied lives. Some people say it shortened the war by many months and perhaps even years.

The Holocaust

Adolf Hitler

Adolf Hitler hated Jewish people and he believed that they had no right to live. As soon as the Nazis took power in Germany in 1933 they attacked German Jews. They removed all their legal rights, ruined their businesses and destroyed their synagogues. Many Jews fled abroad in fear of their lives.

The yellow star

In 1939, the Nazis forced German Jews to sew a yellow star on to their clothes so that they could be easily identified. By 1942, every Jew in occupied Europe was ordered to wear a yellow star.

The 'Final Solution'

During the war, Germany occupied Poland and several other countries where many Jews lived. Some were herded together in ghettos in the big towns. Others were sent to concentration camps – types of prisons where they were badly treated and often worked to death. Hundreds of thousands of Jews were shot or gassed in mobile gas vans. In January 1942, Nazi leaders met to plan what Hitler called 'the final solution of the Jewish question'; the death of all European Jews. Six concentration camps were set up in eastern Europe. Jews were brought to these camps by train and killed in gas chambers. Their bodies were then burned. The most notorious of these six camps was Auschwitz in Nazi-occupied Poland.

Anne Frank

Anne Frank was a German-born Jew who grew up in Amsterdam in the Netherlands. After the Nazi invasion in 1940, her family hid in a room above her father's office. In August 1944, they were betrayed and sent to Auschwitz. Anne died just before the war ended, but her diary was published in 1947. In it, Anne wrote about her experiences of hiding during the war.

The death toll

The total number of Jews killed in these camps and all across Europe was almost 6 million. More than 1.1 million Jews were killed at Auschwitz alone. This terrible event is known as the Holocaust. The Jewish people call it the *Shoah*, from the Hebrew word for 'catastrophe'. It was, and remains, one of the worst acts of genocide in world history.

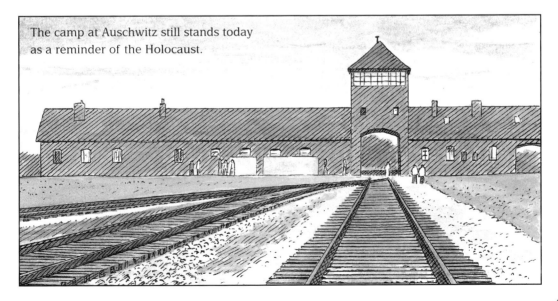

The camp at Auschwitz still stands today as a reminder of the Holocaust.

The Battle of Kursk

After their victory at Stalingrad, the Soviet Red Army had gained the advantage. The Germans were forced back from Moscow in the centre and out of the Caucasus in the south. In July 1943, the two armies met at Kursk in central Russia.

Red victory

The Red Army had managed to make progress and advanced into the German lines around the railway junction at Kursk. The Germans tried to force their lines back. They sent out 2,928 tanks, 2,110 aircraft and 780,900 men. Opposing them were larger numbers: 5,128 Soviet tanks, 2,792 aircraft and almost 2 million members of the Red Army.

The Soviet T-34 tank was faster and could go further than its German counterpart. This was a significant factor in the Soviet victory at Kursk.

The event became one of the biggest ever tank battles in history. The Germans attacked on 5 July and were met with a massive Soviet counter-attack on 12 July. Losses were huge on both sides. On one day alone, the Germans lost more than 300 tanks. By 15 July the Red Army had won. German losses were so great they were unable to mount another major attack in the USSR.

Pushing west

After Kursk, the Red Army fought its way westwards towards Germany. It cleared German troops out of Ukraine, the Crimea and central Russia. The siege of Leningrad was lifted in January 1944. And in a massive campaign from June to August of 1944, known as Operation Bagration, the Red Army finally cleared the Germans out of the USSR for good.

The Invasion of Italy

After success in north Africa, the Allies invaded Italy. On 10 July 1943, troops landed in Sicily. Mussolini was overthrown and the new Italian government surrendered to the Allies. Allied troops then landed in southern Italy, but before they could advance very far German troops occupied the country. They rescued Mussolini and set him up as the head of a new government.

A hard fight

The battle for Italy was hard. For eighteen months, the Allies had to fight their way up the mainland mile by mile. In January 1944, the Allies established a beachhead – a temporary line of defence – at Anzio. After a desperate fight, they managed to break out into the countryside south of Rome. At the same time, a lengthy five-month battle began to capture the hilltop monastery at Monte Cassino, a key point in the German line of defence.

Slow progress

When Allied troops entered Rome on 4 June 1944, the Germans withdrew without a fight. The Allies were halfway up the mainland of Italy, but it was only when Germany finally surrendered in 1945 that all of Italy was liberated.

ITALY 1943-44

Monte Cassino was eventually captured in May 1944 by 50,000 Polish troops. They wanted revenge for the German occupation of their country.

D-Day

On the night of 5–6 June 1944, a vast Allied fleet set sail from the south coast of England across the English Channel. The fleet headed for Normandy in France. There, the troops landed in the early morning of 6 June, D-Day. The invasion was known as Operation Overlord. It was the first stage in a plan to liberate France and defeat Nazi Germany.

A vast fleet

The invasion fleet was the biggest ever in naval history. More than 150,000 American, British and Canadian troops crossed the Channel. They sailed in 75 convoys of 6,500 naval craft, supported by 12,000 aircraft. Two artificial harbours were then towed across the Channel to provide safe ports. An oil pipeline was run under the sea from England to provide much needed fuel for tanks and trucks in France.

The first troops ashore made the beaches as safe as possible before the equipment was unloaded from the ships.

Victory

The landings were successful. Allied troops met fierce opposition from the Germans in Normandy but broke out into the rest of France on 25 July. Paris was liberated on 25 August. In the same month, US troops invaded the south of France and swept northwards. By the end of the year, Allied troops had liberated the whole of France and Belgium and stood on the banks of the River Rhine.

The Normandy beaches

The Allies gave names to the five Normandy beaches they landed on. The British landed on Sword and Gold beaches and the Canadians on Juno. The Americans landed on Omaha and Utah beaches. Omaha is the largest city in the US state of Nebraska; Utah is a US state.

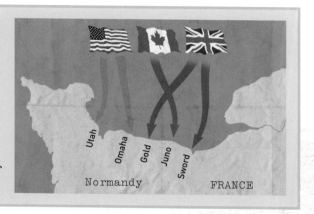

The Defeat of Germany

ALLIED OCCUPATION OF GERMANY IN 1945

In early 1945, Allied troops entered western Germany. They crossed the River Rhine and spread out across the country. To the east, Soviet troops invaded Poland and liberated the Balkans and Hungary. They then headed to Berlin, the German capital. American troops met Red Army troops coming in the other direction – the first time the two allies' troops had met during the war.

The fall of Berlin

On 25 April 1945, after two and half years of non-stop fighting all the way from Stalingrad, the Red Army troops surrounded Berlin. They bombed the city and stormed into the centre. On 30 April, Adolf Hitler killed himself in his underground bunker. Fighting continued for a few more days until the Germans finally surrendered on 7 May 1945.

Red Reichstag

On 2 May 1945, two Russian soldiers raised the Soviet flag over the ruined Reichstag, the parliament building in Berlin. This has come to be seen as a very significant moment at the end of the war, as it symbolized the end of Nazi rule in Germany.

VE (Victory in Europe) Day was celebrated on 8 May 1945. After six years of fighting, the guns were silent and Europe was at peace again.

Final Defeat

Although the war against Germany ended in May 1945, it dragged on against Japan for another three months. When the end came, it was very sudden.

Towards Japan

Throughout 1943 and 1944, the Americans had steadily pushed the Japanese back across the Pacific Ocean. US troops landed in the Philippines in October 1944 and defeated a large Japanese naval fleet at Leyte Gulf. In January 1945, they attacked the main island of Luzon. The Japanese resisted fiercely, killing thousands of US troops before surrendering. Attacks against the small Japanese islands of Iwo Jima and Okinawa led to massive loss of life on both sides. It was clear to the Americans that any invasion of the Japanese mainland would result in the death of many thousands of their troops.

Atomic bombs

By now, US bombers were able to target Japanese cities. They bombed Tokyo and other cities. On 6 August 1945, the Americans dropped a new and secret weapon on Hiroshima – an atomic bomb. Three days later, they dropped another bomb on Nagasaki. Both cities were totally destroyed and thousands were killed. On 14 August 1945, the Japanese emperor surrendered, overruling his military leaders. When the emperor broadcast the news to the Japanese people, it was the first time any of them had ever heard his voice.

The damage caused by the atomic explosions was devastating.
Almost all of the buildings in Hiroshima and Nagasaki were totally destroyed.

Atomic destruction

The two atomic bombs dropped on Japanese cities caused immense destruction. Huge fireballs and a massive shock wave killed tens of thousands of people and flattened the centres of both Hiroshima and Nagasaki. Many more people then died of radiation sickness over the next five years. It is estimated that 270,000 people lost their lives in Hiroshima alone.

The Impact of the War

At least 60 million people lost their lives in the Second World War. The USSR alone lost 27 million people. Poland lost 5 million people, one fifth of its pre-war population. Many towns and cities were bombed flat. Millions of people lost their homes and jobs and millions more became refugees.

Armed peace

The two most powerful wartime allies – the USA and USSR – soon fell out. The two countries opposed each other's political systems and a 'cold war', where no direct military conflict took place, existed between them until the USSR collapsed in 1991. Europe remained at peace, but was divided by an 'iron curtain'. Germany was split in two – American and British troops occupied the west; Soviet troops occupied the east. As Democratic governments were re-established across western Europe, Communists took control in the east.

War crimes

Some of the Nazi leaders disappeared after the war or killed themselves. But twenty-one were prosecuted for war crimes at Nuremberg in Germany. Eleven were sentenced to death. In Japan, seven leaders were hanged and sixteen more imprisoned for life. In Germany, the Nazi Party was made illegal and Nazis excluded from public life.

International co-operation

Two organizations owe their existence to the war. In 1945, the Allied nations set up the United Nations. It helps the world's nations try to settle their disagreements peacefully. In 1957, France, Germany and four other countries set up a European Economic Community (now the European Union). France and Germany had fought each other three times in seventy years and now wanted to work together peacefully.

The Second World War is still remembered today. Many of those who lost their lives are buried in huge cemeteries close to the scenes of conflict. In remembering the war, we all hope that it will never happen again.

Key Figures of the War

It would be impossible to mention all the people who had a significant impact on the Second World War; there are far too many. These are some of the key figures who were involved in events or who made decisions that changed the course of the war.

**Winston Churchill
(1874–1965)**
British prime minister
from 1940 to the end
of the war

**Charles de Gaulle
(1890–1970)**
Leader of the Free French
movement from 1940,
later president of France

**General Dwight D.
Eisenhower (1890–1969)**
Supreme Allied
Commander of the D-Day
invasion of Europe in 1944

**Anne Frank
(1929–1945)**
Jewish girl who was
hidden in Nazi-occupied
Amsterdam

**George VI
(1895–1952)**
British wartime king,
who reigned from
1936 to 1952

**Hermann Goering
(1893–1946)**
Nazi commander of
the Luftwaffe
(German air force)

**Heinrich Himmler
(1900–1945)**

Nazi leader who was the
main organizer of
the Holocaust

**Emperor Hirohito
(1901–1989)**

Emperor of Japan from
1926; he accepted Allied
peace terms in 1945

**Adolf Hitler
(1889–1945)**

Chancellor of Germany
from 1933 and
Nazi leader

**Benito Mussolini
(1883–1945)**

Leader of Italy from 1922;
overthrown in 1943 and
later shot by partisans

**General Erwin Rommel
(1891–1944)**

German commander in
Africa until his defeat at
El Alamein

**Franklin D. Roosevelt
(1882–1945)**

US president from
1933 until his death
in April 1945

**Josef Stalin
(1878–1953)**

Leader of the USSR
from 1924 until his
death in 1953

**Harry S. Truman
(1884–1972)**

US vice-president to
Roosevelt, who succeeded
him in April 1945

**Marshal Georgy Zhukhov
(1896–1974)**

Soviet leader of the
Red Army

Timeline of Main Events

1939

22 May	Pact of Steel signed between Germany and Italy
23 August	Germany signs non-aggression pact with USSR and agrees to divide Poland between the two countries
1 September	Germany invades Poland, followed later by USSR
3 September	Britain and France declare war on Germany, the Second World War begins
15 September	Japan signs peace agreement with USSR

1940

April–May	Germany invades Denmark, Norway, Holland, Belgium, Luxembourg and France
10 May	Winston Churchill becomes British prime minister
26 May–4 June	British troops are evacuated from Dunkirk, France
10 June	Italy declares war on Britain and France
21 June	France surrenders and is occupied
10 July	Battle of Britain begins
7 September	Start of the Blitz against British cities
9–16 September	Italy invades British-run Egypt
27 September	Germany, Italy and Japan sign the tri-partite pact
31 October	Battle of Britain ends

1941

6 April	Germany invades Yugoslavia and Greece
22 June	Germany invades the USSR
15 September	Siege of Leningrad begins
7 December	Japan attacks US naval base at Pearl Harbor and invades south-east Asia, USA joins the war on the British side

1942

20 January	Nazis meet at the Wannsee Conference to plan the destruction of all European Jews
15 February	British base at Singapore surrenders to the Japanese
8 May	US fleet defeats Japanese fleet in the Coral Sea
30 May	Britain launches a 1,000-bomber raid against the German city of Cologne
6 June	Important US naval victory at Midway Island
8 November	Operation Torch begins as Allied troops invade north-west Africa

1943

31 January	Massive German defeat at Stalingrad
12 May	German troops surrender in north Africa
30 June	US begins Operation Cartwheel to clear Japanese from Pacific islands
5–15 July	Soviet victory in huge tank battle at Kursk
3 September	Allies invade Italy; Mussolini overthrown
13 October	Italy declares war on Germany

1944

June–August	Operation Bagration clears Germans out of the USSR
4 June	Allies capture Rome
6 June	D-Day invasion of Europe by the Allies
15 August	In Operation Anvil US troops land in the south of France
25 August	Allies liberate Paris
17 October	US troops invade Philippines
23–26 October	Massive Japanese naval defeat in Leyte Gulf, Philippines

1945

12 January	Red Army crosses into Germany
17 January	Red Army enters Warsaw
27 January	Red Army liberates Auschwitz
13–15 February	Allied firebombing of Dresden
7 March	Allies cross the Rhine at Remagen
26 March	US troops capture Japanese island of Iwo Jima
12 April	US president Roosevelt dies; Harry Truman takes over
25 April	Red Army surrounds Berlin; Soviet and American troops meet for first time
28 April	Mussolini killed by Italian partisans
30 April	Hitler kills himself
2 May	Fighting ends in Italy
7 May	Germany surrenders
8 May	VE – Victory in Europe – Day
6 August	Atomic bomb dropped on Hiroshima
8 August	USSR declares war on Japan and invades Manchuria
9 August	Atomic bomb dropped on Nagasaki
14 August	Japan surrenders
15 August	VJ – Victory in Japan – Day

Glossary

alliance formal agreement between two or more friendly countries that have the same aims

Allies, the Britain and France and their empires, the USA, USSR, China and other countries who joined forces to fight the Axis nations

ally country linked with another by a treaty or friendship

armistice ceasefire agreement that stops a war

arms weapons, vehicles or machinery used to fight a war

auxiliary providing a supporting role, often to the armed services

Axis, the Germany, Italy, Japan and other countries who fought on the same side during the war

blitzkrieg fierce German military campaign

bomber military aeroplane designed to drop bombs

civilian person who is not in the military or connected with them

code system of letters and symbols that replaces the words of a message, making it secure

code-breaking ability to read an enemy's coded messages

colony country or region controlled by another country as part of an empire

communist	person or group that believes in a society in which everyone is equal and all property is owned by the state
convoy	fleet of merchant ships escorted by armed warships to protect them from enemy attack
curfew	restriction on movement at night
dictator	leader who takes complete control of a country and rules by force
dogfight	close combat between two fighter planes
empire	group of different countries ruled by one nation and its emperor
fighter	fast military aircraft designed to fight enemy aircraft in the skies
genocide	deliberate killing of a group or nation of people
ghetto	part of a city or town where Jews were forced to live
Holocaust, **the**	German plan to kill all Jewish people
liberate	set a state or people free from another ruler
merchant ship	ship that carries goods and supplies
Nazi Party	National Socialist Party, which was led by Adolf Hitler and ruled Germany from 1933 to 1945

Glossary

pact   agreement between two or more countries

partisan   member of an armed resistance group
                      fighting from within a country against
                      an occupying army

prime minister   head of an elected government, such as
                      in Britain

rationing   weekly allowance of food and supplies

Red Army, the   Soviet army, so-called because of the red
                      Soviet flag

refugee   someone fleeing their country for political
                      or other reasons

resistance   fighting back against an enemy

sniper   military gunman who fires from a hidden
                      place at individual enemy soldiers

squadron   large number of military aircraft or ships

surrender   to give in to a superior force and
                      stop fighting

swastika   ancient Indian symbol used by the Nazis

sympathizer   person who supports another person
                      or cause

treaty   formal agreement between one or
                      more countries

U-boat   German 'underwater ship' or submarine

Places to Visit

Bletchley Park, Milton Keynes, Buckinghamshire
Chartwell, Kent, home of Winston Churchill
Chislehurst Caves, Chislehurst, Kent
Churchill War Rooms, London
HMS Belfast, London
Imperial War Museum Duxford, Cambridgeshire
Imperial War Museum North, Manchester
Imperial War Museum London, London
National Army Museum, London
Second World War Experience Centre, Leeds
The Tank Museum, Dorset

For more information about the Second World War and
other resources, visit **www.ladybird.com**

Index